The Last Day

Krikor Der Hohannesian

Červená Barva Press
Somerville, Massachusetts

Červená Barva Press
P.O. Box 440357
W. Somerville, MA 02144-3222

www.cervenabarvapress.com

Bookstore: www.thelostbookshelf.com

Cover art: "City Landscape" by Garabed Der Hohannesian

Cover design: William J. Kelle

ISBN: 978-1-950063-20-8

"The Last Day" is dedicated to my long-time partner, Judith Kneen, whose encouragement, praise and constructive commentary for my poetry has been so appreciated over the years.

TABLE OF CONTENTS

The Last Day

CONVERSATION

Mind was bored one day
so he decided to play
with what it would be like
to be completely bored,
as in dead. But the rest of mind
fired up a barrage of flak,
cacophony enough
to startle heart,
who was in the midst
of an afternoon nap
What the hell was that?
yells heart.

Well, says mind, there's
this little corner of me
that's curious but, trust me,
I don't go there very often
much less stay long. That's
what we minds do, go to weird
places now and then. Sometimes
I'd rather be you – all heart,
so I don't have to think
about such things. Well,
says heart, you needn't worry.
I'm the one who should be afraid.
If I stop I won't be able to
feel ever again. I don't know
anything else - I'd be lost. Besides,
surprise!, I enjoy our arguments!
Don't you see, says mind,
that's the point. When you stop
what happens to me? I'll have
no one to play with and
I was just trying to imagine
what that might be like.
By now, mind has a headache.
Welcome to my world says heart,
I get it. If you go dead before me

what's the use of carrying on?
They have these contraptions
that keep me thumping whether
you're there or not. If you leave
I don't trust others to decide.
If you're gone, I want to go with you.
Says mind, far too morose
dear heart. Tomorrow is
tomorrow, how about
some Coltrane and a growler or two?
Heart leaps, riffs a quick jig step –
you're on, my friend!

REQUIESCAT IN PACE

East Parish Cemetery, 1950

We visited often,
just the two of us,
always at night –
what drew us, God
knows. Back then

some snickered –
just a farrago of moldered bones
sleeping off eternity. From friends,
at least, the question etched
on quizzical brows, Why?

But the darkness was alive!
The barn owl's hoot,
yellow eyes on watch.
Small paws rustling -
chipmunks, raccoons,
skunks on midnight rounds.
Bats wooshing the sepulchral air,
the soft October fog a muted lament.
The wind's December sighs
through skeletal oak and maple

And the markers –
from simple granite stones
and marble obelisks to
ornate vaults engraved
with names, dates, alive
with family sagas. Here,
the history of three centuries
interred in shadowed silence
and we wondered,
Who were you?

BIRD OF PREY

The wind is down
at the hour of change,
light to dark. A vacuum
of eerie quiet, weightless
on the shoulders, the nape
of the neck, the usual squawk
and bustle of feeding time
absent – something is up…

Against the backdrop
of crepuscular light,
the Norway maple's branches,
unbudded, reach for what
can't be retrieved, the waning
of the light. Its silhouetted veins
stretch toward a rising gibbous moon
flanked by the wink of Venus and Jupiter.

In the highest branch, the hawk,
        perched, black as La Brea tar,
                still as the midnight to come,
                        sentinel for the coming dark.

He waits…the minutes crawl.
I envy him, his patience,
The calm of knowing he'll get
what he needs, tho'

not tonight, his prey vanished
        their own instinct on high alert.

Of a sudden serrated wings slice
    the night air on a glide path,
        a graceful swoop toward dawn's promise
            some creature, unwitting, living its last night.

WALKING

I.

I thought of you, nene,
  when I read of the discovery -
    a remote cave,
      an obscure province,
        Vayots Dzor, Armenia.

The world's oldest shoe,
        predating Otzi the Iceman's,
            unearthed - preserved
              in sheep dung and dried grass
                for five millennia.

Who would have thought
              to dig there?

II.

Family legend has it
        that you walked from Aintab
            to Constantinople, in defiance
                of tradition and gender,
                  your ambition to be a teacher.

I confess my skepticism –
        five hundred miles?

But then that steely look
    lips pursed, a taut line,
      when you spoke of the Turks,
        the forced shoe-less death marches
          over Deir-al-Zor's scorched sands
            where so many fell along the way, feet
blistered, energy sapped by unquenched thirst.

Yes, we Armenians
         are long-accustomed
                to walking - for survival
                           if for nothing else.

RESURRECTION

Salt Lake City, Utah

Askew in a grimy corner
propped with other remnants,
an estate's unwanted detritus
minutes from a funereal trip
to the salt flats,

   "Still Life with Grapes"

luscious with bluish purple of Merlot,
garnet of Cabernet, lime green of Chenin,
catches a curious eye – a legacy rescued
for a pittance from the graveyard
of forgotten art.

As for the artist, my father,
ashes long since scattered to the wind,
his spirit breathes a sigh of relief.

Ah, the vagaries of art!

THE CHERRY TREE
Aintab, Cilicia

Forgotten corner of the caliphate,
mother's birthplace, she
uprooted at two, a tramp steamer
to Salonika - otherwise another statistic
in the million and a half or, worse,
a concubine in some pasha's seraglio.

Cousin Anahid went back,
the family home survives .
She is eager to describe. Her mother
made the trip at 100, her voice
awash in weeping the entire stay.

Don't tell me, I plead.
The pomegranate trees, the bushes
hunched with pistachios, the smell of lamb
spit-roasted, the line dancing,
the happy voices –
it all disappears if you tell me.

Pamuk says Armenian houses in Kars
are ghost houses, haunted by specters
that wail bloody murder. One by one
the last of those who survived April, 1915,
pass on – the thread frays to a wisp.

Five decades I have pondered going back -
Would I spit on the first Turk I saw?
Tell me to my face you still deny it! Tell me!

But I fear the ghosts. I fear mourning
what was never mine , the grief
that belongs not to me but to those
who gave up their birthright. Instead,

to those who survive, instructions:
till my ashes into the patch at Mt. Auburn

where their bones molder. *Wait*
'til April, I say, *the cherry tree*
rooted to their graves
will be in full bloom then.

SHRINKAGE

He had fallen again
but this time failed to rise,
the hangman's fracture,
the one that kills instantly when
the trapdoor yawns and the noose
jerks your head up. It would have
been a blessing – instead
he spat in death's face once more...

to what avail?
Month after month,
his Parkinson's-riddled body
shrunken more each day –
matchstick legs that would never walk again,
gnarled hands, fingers unable
to lift spoon to mouth
or pick up a telephone, the halting
ever more sibilant speech.

the litany of complaints about his caregivers
   who combed his hair
      bathed him, shaved him
        wiped his ass
          brushed his teeth
            balmed his bedsores
              fed him thrice daily

Yet he fought on...
"Goddammit, if Joe Bach (107 years old)
      can walk so can I...",

I saw his hunger for normalcy...

wanting to go out to lunch
...a couple of beers for old time's sake...

  or one last visit to the old neighborhood,

the glint in his eyes, smile
      nascent at the corners, whenever
            a young lady entered his room…

Who was I to question his fantasies,
      his stubbornness in the face of demise?

I wanted to talk about death,
      he talked of going home –

more and more he lacked words,
      the life in his eyes waning,
          breath stertorous, labored –
the angel of death
      ahover that last night, waiting
          to claim dominion.

Staying present all that was left,
  as one by one the family ranks thin,
    an army in retreat
      as if to live to fight another day -
        as if there was a war
          still to be waged and won.

THE DAY APPROACHING
in memory of Mara Stevenson

As sudden as a summer squall
the prognosis eclipses the sun,
a cloud of surety that your days
will never again be the same.

Of a sudden, life is rudely finite and
the question "if you knew tomorrow
was your last day…" isn't the grist
of cocktail party chatter. Instead,

    days of suffering

days of hope

    days of despair

counting down
against the allotment,
loosening the fierce
grip on days now
precious as pearls.

New Year's Eve and
oyster bisque - no
one could make it
better than you- *"My Old
Kentucky Home,"* loud,
soulful at midnight.

SOUL BROTHER

We celebrated for three days,
chewed on stories, grooved with Paul Robeson,
Joe Cocker, Jimmy Cliff, Louis Armstrong,
got down and dusty on baby backs, collards,
dirty rice, sweet potato pie. Drowned the blues
in drink, raised the rafters with hallelujahs.

The day-after tears - not the choked back kind but
full-bore gushing – finally swamped me
like a rogue wave. I am lost,
marooned on an isle of mourning. Dusk
falls in silence, I grope the gloom
for solace, praying for grace. It is late fall -
a rising gibbous moon backlights skeletal maple,
the marigolds rust and wilt, squirrels rustle
leaves burying winter caches, fallen apples
rot to their cores, geese in v-formation
intent on climes more clement.

You shouldn't have left so soon, there are things
not finished. We were to be octogenarians together,
to be the wisest of the wise – wiser than Solomon,
filled with more stories than the eldest griot.

You shouldn't have left so suddenly, there
are things yet unsaid, inchoate raps in need
of ripening - never mind proper farewells.

Tomorrow's forecast is inclement. I shall write
your epitaph, as asked, and weep some more
in concert with the rain. In December days
perhaps the cold will numb but I will feel
mortality's sleety sting against a frozen face.

Come March, April the crocuses' yellows
and purples will not be quite so brilliant,
the grass shoots not quite so verdant,
the mockingbirds' trills and runs

a shade short of their usual bravura.
I shall dig holes for plantings nonetheless.

IF THE EGRET COULD SPEAK

The photograph, a gusher of truth –
the lone egret, tarred and feathered,
forlorn on the despoiled beach, tears
of black ooze dripping from wings
no longer able to fly, to swoop for
sustenance in the sulphured estuary –
scant days from death. I imagine
being stripped of primal instinct,
the urge to take wing, to dive and fish.
Death, then, brings freedom, a cleansing.
Sadness engulfs me – heavy,
crude and angry. And if the egret
could speak? Might it tell the story
of man doing unnatural things,
boring the ocean floor four miles deep,
the arrogance of it all?

REQUIEM

Mother, dear Mother – last of those from home –
with your final raspy breath the eternal flame
shivered briefly with remembrance for all those
whose blood has long since dried to dust, whose
mutilated bones augment the scree upon rock-strewn
plateaus where once our forebears grazed sheep,
gathered pistachios, harvested figs and grapes.

In the shadow of Ararat, churches of by-gone Byzantine grandeur
molder on once fertile plains now barren of a way of life. The wind
whistles through where sublime frescoes and stained glass once
    glowed –
testaments to the glories of God, now only a memorial
to His departed flock.

Almost a century has passed, fresh rumors float on the wind. .
Osman's descendants intend to plow under
all vestiges, once and for all to silence the screams,
the pleading, the cursing against a forsaking God,
the raging against their butchers by ghostly spirits.

Ah, but for the Brutus in their midst, so they might assuage
guilt, expunge sins, bury the lies. Anatolian breezes
will forever betray them, bearing bone dust
and blood motes into every fissure and crevice
where Armenians once lived.

Where you, Mother, once lived.

AT THE 50TH
Harvard College Reunion, Class of 1958

Adrift between symposia and seminars,
a drizzle of reverie on Bow Street,
aimless nostalgia graying in droplets of fog.
At the corner of Arrow the campanile
of St. Paul's looming through the mist,
Italianate monolith, blood- red brick.

this was where you fell, Marco,
a bluster of a June day, 1957, the day
the scaffolding betrayed you, left
you hanging to mock gravity, the split
second of wonder before the inevitable.

I stare up, watch the swallows and wrens
loop and hover about the belfry clock,
the minute hand inches toward the hour,
the bells toll three, the birds
whoosh off at the plangent peal.

that was when you fell, after sweaty
hours sandblasting brick,
flailing the humid air, wingless
against the corkscrew dive.

I stare down at the concrete
where your blood once pooled –
so where were the winged angels
to waft you safely to ground?

they said your head hit first,
that the sound was one nobody
would want to hear again.

And tonight we will be dining and
dancing – a cloudburst of reminiscence
for us who have survived the thunder
of a half century, the one lost to you

19

in a heart's single beat,
a rogue gust of hot wind.

CASA de la LUZ

Nothing more could be done, so
on a bright desert morning they came.

Your home, existential oasis, where
you intended to stay to the very last,
the trailer with its "gate to nowhere", plunked
amid the saguaro, prickly pear and tumbleweed,
where never again would you lay your head
under star-studded nights. Where feral cats
would not find supper put out at six sharp,
the marijuana patch would wither of thirst
and the four vintage Volkswagens begin to rust
in the desert dust – Tobacco Road in Arizona.
Kerouac, favored apostle, would have bowed –
On the road, morphine and ativan,
the final leg – Casa de la Luz,

House of Light, adobe and terra cotta,
angelic statuary beaded in turquoise,
the last way station before road-less eternity.
Down to a few days, the sleep of the dying,
sister and long-lost son on vigil –
chanting, waiting. Clear Light Lady said

"follow the breath, breathe with him,
bathe him in a boundless ocean of light,
when you hear the change it will be hours –
do not hold his hand then, he needs to let go"

On the fifth night I dreamt of a bird,
white as alabaster, paragon of grace
winging off into a night sky –
disappearing into indigo. Pre-dawn,
your in-breath shallower,
the exhale raspy and guttural,
halting. Sun-up, three loud breaths, then
silence, a settled hush, a wisp of a breeze

flutters the curtains. You, unfettered,
a fresh memory stripped of its flesh.

BLOOD

To our question

What happened?

the answer was

Blood

Blood in the Araxes, blood
in Lake Van, blood in the Caucasus,
in the valleys, in the high plains
of Anatolia, blood in the town squares
of every village, blood of pregnant
mothers, of babies, aunts and uncles,
brothers and sisters, *mairigs* and *hairigs*,
no souls spared – the "Armenian Question",
hatred's euphemism, settled once and for all.
Or so they thought, except
enough survived and it is their blood
that courses the deltas of our veins. They hadn't
counted on that, they hadn't reckoned
that blood carries memory downstream.

They killed a Turkish consul in Union Square
some years ago, his blood spattered all over
the windshield and dashboard – forty or more
bullets it was rumored. They did the same
in Vienna and Paris in the cause
of acknowledgement and birthed
my dirty little secret – a frisson
of satisfaction, an ephemeral vengeance.

But, my children, it isn't as simple
as damming up sadness or letting loose
a geyser of rage. Almost a century,
and my heart still bleeds into the river,
on and on it flows to the ocean,

23

all judgment pickled
in bloodied brine.

SMALL DEATHS

a phone call in the middle of the night,
the son of a best friend – words
choked by the heave of sobs
erupting from his belly – his father,
a sudden death, and the air whooshes
from my lungs, but no words come…

or others, friends you once
danced and sang with,
still on this earth but many
now lame or raspy-voiced

and you, sister, children
a continent away, living
with angst and two Abyssinians
your comfort at night

or you, brother, your gait
shuffled by the disease
that one day not so distant
has claim on you

or you, dearest, your mother's
ship long since having left port
on a tide of dementia and you
on the shore still waving
safe journey, safe journey…

and so I watch the insults
pile up and give them names,
like "Arthur" for arthritis, "Nolan"
for no language as I search
for a lost word, "Stenny" for stenosis
when my legs don't work quite right.

All this we might call aging,
these losses one by one,
or we might call them small deaths,

a collective prelude, as if one's own demise
will be the symphony of all symphonies.

WAKE

Ifeanyi Mankiti, in memorium

How absolute, permanent
the stillness of death…

I stood beside your casket
willing to stay as long as it took
to see your chest rise and fall again,
wishing your eyes to open,
your lips to part in speech,
signature smile at the corners,
waiting to see your hand reach out
as if to reassure us all.

I wanted to break with decorum,
extend my hand to touch yours
as you touched so many,
propriety be damned!

ONE BY ONE

One by one
they have left port,
its bustle of life,
sails luffed, set out
into the wind of forever,
over the horizon toward
the harbor none of us can know,
know only there is no return,
a scar of grief on the hearts
of those left behind.

Now, in these days of
more frequent partings
a reminder that my turn
is not far off.

When my day arrives,
come to the quay, dear ones.
If I haven't yet left, squeeze
my hand, let us shed
salty tears, a last smile
for what bound us all. Or,
if my ship has sailed, linger
a while, smell the fresh salt air,
let the wind caress your face,
dry your tears, and may the warmth
of the sun bless your day. I
will be a dot on the far horizon.
Look for me, remember,
I will be waving.

SAYING GOODBYE

He had been wilting
like the frost-touched
chrysanthemum in late October
only it was now April when
forsythia trumpeted new life
in a song-burst of yellow blossoms.

The call from the hospital –
the voice solemn as a preacher's,
*your father's heart, his breathing
has stopped, we are keeping him alive.*
A flood of memories and feelings
compressed into an hour's drive,
the tide of a life ebbing.

The drip of the IV, the beep-beep
of the monitors, the hiss of
the respirator, his eyes open
veiled with the film of death.
His lips moving, soundless,
there was nothing left to say.

I opened my mouth, no words.
*No, pops, the unsaid shall stay
unsaid – the ache of old scars
freshened, the chasm of the years.
It can't be helped in the few hours left.*
Only instructions remained:
do not resuscitate – it wasn't long.

Mother didn't believe in funerals –
after all, none of the 1.5 million
dispatched by the Ottomans were so graced.
She was two years old and had survived.
Do what you need to do.

He, the artist, who graced me
with a love of the aesthetic. Whatever

his failings, this was no small thing.
I arranged the cremation – the least
I could do, the proper goodbye
to quench the fire that had consumed us.
I scattered his ashes at Lighthouse Beach,
the sand cool and damp, left it to the tide
to deposit them wherever it might.

NARCISSUS

treat every day as if it were your last...

O, the banality! -
as if one could cram in all yet undone,
wishes fulfilled helter-skelter, then sigh
and happily give up the ghost.

Once, all seemed possible,
    without boundary.
In the heyday of youth's fields,
infinite tomorrows beckoned
beyond the day's horizon.

Ah, but the ravages of aging
have done their dirty deeds!
I want the mirror to lie,
conceit to blot truth -

you're looking good, chappie...

and then the ghostly whisper,

(for your age)...

Would the same have befallen
Narcissus left untempted
by the wiles of Nemesis?
Was he lucky to die young,
still smitten with his reflection?

And if today were to be the last?

I look in the mirror, its pool
of reflected reality -
jagged creases, saggy jowls,
pouched eyes, trying
to imagine myself
no longer here.

THE WANING OF THE LIGHT
for Patrick Seyon

The light is crepuscular
in the shrunken world
of his bedroom, his life
now in twilight.

I see it in his eyes,
those eyes that once
effervesced with
    humor and wit,
      intelligence and curiosity,
          a mere hint of glimmer now.

I see it in his Parkinson's- riddled body,
    clenched fists, rigid legs, the struggle
      of his brain to produce a word or two.

His brow furrows,
a mind still at work
words or no. I am left
to guess his thoughts.

I ask questions, see
his lips attempt to move
with answers, watch his eyelids
droop, betray his frustration.
He is down to "yes" and "no".

I grasp his hands in mine,
a faint smile crosses his lips,
then gone, eyes closed.

He sleeps,

My grip relaxes.

LAND CRUISE

Not even a presidential appeal
will sway me today
this first warm day of May –
planet earth's reserves
be damned. Along the roadside
all has leapt awake
from winter's sleep. Sunbursts
of forsythia dazzle the eye,
flowering crabs explode
into giant sherbert cones, saliva
bubbles at the corners of a smile.

Only days ago elm, maple
and oak but tangled masses
of bare ribs – now by miracle
in full blossom, great fans
of green silk, buoyant in the wind,
deploy invisible legions of pollen –
torture bloodshot eyes.

A funeral cortege creeps past,
casts its shadow. Solemn sprays
of gladiolus are on display, windshields
cradle the sun's reflection masking
tearful faces. The headlights
are on high beam but
the grillwork does not smile.

THE MOMENT

Somewhere you wait, silent
companion life-long at my elbow
in this rutted trek we share.
Make no mistake – I've
had it easy. I have loved
and been loved, belly never
knifed by starvation's pangs
nor psyche dealt the torment
of those wishing harm.
I have played and danced and sung,
laughed and wept, praised and cursed.

Yet this need to know you!
To see you as friend
not mysterious foe,
to imagine you under a cherry tree
as blood red fruit, fully ripe, falls
to your lap, to picture you lolling
on a deserted beach soaked
in the warmth of a July sun
rivulets of salt-blue high tide
washing over your feet - your smile
smug in knowing that you
have last dance.

How will you come to me?
A knocking at the door, soft
and undemanding or hard
and insistent? Guest at my table
or unwanted intruder? Or will
I come to you? This

I cannot know. I can but pray
we lock arms when
the moment is upon us
to walk, not in dread,
but with wonder through
the black-veiled portal.

THE LAST DAY

"So whence the world's beauty? Was I deceived?"
John Updike — December 11, 2008

When I lie on that last bed
    on that last night, what
        might I wonder?

Whether I was deceived
    and, if so by whom?
        or was I my own Judas?

The one who pretends
    things are not as they seem,
    that there is no beauty
        in this devilish world.

I would have all the evidence
    any man could need if that
        is where I choose to look.

I confess to having travelled
    that stone-strewn road, the one
        awash in a cloudburst of sorrow, ruts
            cut deep from promises not kept.

Beauty has no address
    on this God-forsaken path
        yet we walk it, searching
            for the one house where
                regret no longer resides.

It would be easy to choose instinct,
    to run like a spooked rabbit caught
        in an open field, desperate for cover,
            the beckoning shelter of the tree-line.

Or I could remember watching
    my children burst from the womb's comfort,

the sunrise on those days like none other,
    the moon those nights a sliver of a smile
        peeking between silhouetted trees.

TO THE AUTHOR OF MY EPITAPH

Hanging helter-skelter in the closet
a favorite cardigan, color of plum
frayed at the elbows, wide-wale corduroys
worn smooth at the knees...

            these are the clothes I wore

My guitar, coffined,
lies on the floor, the metronome
tick-tocks silent rhythms. Sheets of Sanz,
Giuliani, Calatuyud...

            this is the music I played

One Hundred Years of Solitude,
The Plague, Paradise,
A History of Armenia, The Fall,
Beloved, The Spark of Life...

            these are the books I read

and don't forget to check the shelves,
the dog-eared journals veneered with dust-

            in some you'll find my name

How long does the spirit linger
        like dust motes dancing
                in cones of sunlight
                        before it is all forgotten?

            Reincarnation?

a black cat, sleek,
        amber-eyed
                purring for eternity.

ABOUT THE AUTHOR

Krikor Der Hohannesian's poems have appeared in over 275 literary journals including *The South Carolina Review*, *Atlanta Review*, *Louisiana Literature*, *Connecticut Review*, *Comstock Review* and *Natural Bridge*. He is a five-time Pushcart Prize nominee and author of three books, "Ghosts and Whispers" (Finishing Line Press, 2010), "Refuge in the Shadows" (Červená Barva Press, 2013) and "First Generation" (Dos Madres Press, 2020). "Ghosts and Whispers" was a finalist for the Mass Book awards poetry category in 2011. First Generation was selected as a "must read" by Mass Book Awards in 2021.

www.ingramcontent.com/pod-product-compliance
Lightning Source LLC
Chambersburg PA
CBHW021028090426
42738CB00007B/944